25 Years to Life ....

This is a work of fiction. All of the characters, organizations, and events portrayed in this novel either are products of the author's imagination or are used fictitiously. Any resemblance to actual persons, living or dead is purely coincidental.

Foreword.

To the Author,

Upon reading these poems I can't help but to be in awe. The man yielding this pen so masterfully seems to be worlds away from the guy I met back in college. And yet at the same time, so familiar. Each passage that you read here is a gleaming gem, born of kindness tempered with wisdom. Here you will find the gift of pain transmuted into art. May you be comforted by this work. May you find here the justification to keep your beautiful heart open. And above all else, may you be reminded that where you are now is not necessarily where you will be. Keep choosing to love over and over again.

Love Diamond Cooper

Dedication

This is to the little boy or girl who doesn't think they belong in the world. You are able, powerful, and wonderfully made. I'm hoping this book is only a small token of the debt I intend to pay. I dedicate this to the little boy in me who never thought he had a voice. I dedicate this to anyone who ever felt small, and all who ever felt disenchanted by the world and events taking place beyond your control. Thank you in advance for reading what took me a lifetime up until now to make. I want to dedicate this book to my younger brother Jeremiah who blessed me with the cover of this book that is now my first child.

Acknowledgements

First Thank You God for living out your divine purpose through me. It's because of you I have made it this far and I know you aren't finished with me yet.

I want to thank my family for being my foundation, and for supporting me through this process. I thank God for my mother Kathy and my father Dexter Roberson as parents, I am all that I am because of who you both are. I thank my brothers Desmond, and Jeremiah for pushing me to not be stagnant. Throughout the process each of you played an integral part and partially inspired me in writing some of these poems.

I have a lot of people who have left their mark on me. I went through moments where I felt alienated and my friends checked on me and were right there to assist. I love you and thank you Jose. I love and thank you Tara. I love you and thank you Ezell. I love and thank you Ari. I love and thank you Aija. I love you and thank you Stefan. I love you and thank you Elita. I love you and thank you Nayy. I love you and thank you Rhavin. I love and thank you Scott. I love and thank you Nermina. I love and thank you Scott.I love and thank you Chel. I love and thank you Quayla. I love and thank you Julez. I love and thank you Amber. I love you and thank you Tia. I love and thank you Aaron. I love and thank you Maya. I love and thank you Genevieve. I love and thank you Kerry. I love and thank you Scottie. You all helped me keep perspective during the process on my good and bad days and I will never forget it.

Before reading this book, I want to thank you from the bottom of my heart....

Poverty
Abuse
Neglect
When people meet me
See me
Is that what I project?
Do they think I'm dumb?
Or that I'm a crime suspect
Failing to see that
I have something to protect
My family
My bloodline
Is what I have to protect
Bondage
Chains
Suffering
From the blood of my ancestors
Is what I can't forget
I study
I work
And grow
Until my life is over
For them I am
Forever in their debt

Prosperity
Eternally
Seeking it faithfully
Money can be punishing
But not when you're on the other
Side of the money tree
Abundance
Wealth
Opportunity
Never wanting to feel
Poverty
Anxiety rising
Balance due climbing
Past due timing
Is this my value
That money determines what I'm
Allowed to
Experience out of life
Travel the skies
Avoid strife
I refuse to
Put integrity
Under a dollar bill
Even if I lack the skill
To change my life for the better
Where it really counts
Because my identity
Won't be tied
To a dollar sign amount

There are mountains
I thought I'd never reach
Major peaks I couldn't see
Faced with a label
Based on fables
They banned from cable
It brings me sorrow knowing
To some they think my mind
Isn't stable
I retreat
I don't speak
Fading in the background
Hoping and knowing
Nobody will see

I cry
But I don't want to
In my solitude of my mind
My heart is guarded
Positive feelings departed
I hide
To keep others away
From the pain endured through the days
The years
Of my fears
Laughing, Taunting, Sneering
At the tears I don't show
The anxiety nobody knows
I speak
To try and tell truths
Eyes Diverted, Ears Closing, Larynx
Dropping
My head falls
Reminding me why I sometimes
Don't talk at all
Wisdom to deaf ears
Words gone to waste
My voice and words
Don't have a safe place
To be heard
Silence is what they condemned me to
Suffocation
Is my situation
Thoughts held dear
Mind unclear
It's like I'm screaming
But nobody can hear

911 it's an emergency
Injustice has befallen me
I run and run
Realizing my futility
From my subconscious
Thinking of the details makes me
nauseous
Innocence lost
Heavy costs
His touch felt like needles
His gaze felt like frost
Obedience was my price
To have a normal life
Although this secret brought strife
Until one day it was brought to light
Denial
Betrayal
Hoping for understanding and
compassion
But to no avail
Pathologies
That follow me
Want me to be the victim want me to be
the victim faithfully
To wither and quiver
Moments I'd rather not remember
Seconds I'd rather not relive
Because of a person I almost did not
forgive

Jamal Roberson

Bravery or Scarcity
I walk a path
Often lacking clarity
On why society is hard on me
Why must I be strong
When I feel weak
When I feel scared
"Suck It up"
Coverup
And let your anger flare
I hurt too and cry
But the world doesn't care
My body was made
"To work hard"
Not to nurture
But I came from woman
Fighting your femininity is torture
Because there's no closure

For so long
I wanted to be a song
For you to sing
A cup for you to drink
I've dreamt of this day
My breath was taken away
Before you I was on the brink
But since you've came, I haven't strayed
Dangerous games to be played
The heat that simmers when we collide
The rush of my blood
Let's me know we were meant to collide

If I never felt your tenderness again
My sorrows surely would never end
I'm sure I'd fall apart
Skin like cinnamon
Kisses from heaven
We found our own rhythm
It's past simple infatuation
Since I found you in my imagination
If I missed your kisses
I'd be in pieces
Whenever I see you walk through
The doors to my heart
You pull me from out of the dark
I do like to
Do the things
You want me to do
When you have me in the mood

Killing time
Hearing lies
Million times
Love crosses the line
Behind the veil
Is a tale
Where two lovers won't prevail
One is with off scales
Seeing balance as a mask
But finding love is a task
Hearing truths he won't get past
Seeing and not believing
Relations that will not last
Conflict, turmoil, and despair
Characterize the love in this pair
The other naïve
Clinging to toxic connections
Suffering from infections
But too blind to see
That love is the remedy
Within himself is the key
That he must love himself gently
Passion, Fear, and Anxiety
Isn't all that meets the eyes that see
Lovers fight lovers battle with swords
But it is time to cut these chords
I release you with love and all of my
might
To sever this bond so things can be made
right

Told myself I love you
But was the love really there
Tell myself I needed you
Out of fear
Visions of us Emblazoned
In my consciousness
Eternal internal bliss
Told myself it's okay
But it wasn't meant to be
If it's a lesson I needed to learn
To love sincerely
Without hope, wanting, longing
For returns on my investment
Because love and faith are a testament
To the trials, false starts, tribulations
Can't breakdown
Won't back down
From what love has called me to do
Even if that means losing you

His complexion cinnamon
His hair waved gently
As he talked swiftly
I felt his fire burning intensely
Not knowing him now would be a travesty
Since we couldn't connect before
And now I want to know him forever more
The feeling of a sunset gave me chills
When we first met
I'm never bored
Because it's you adore
Feelings of ecstasy I can't forget
Pushing me to new levels of consciousness
Got my heart palpitating sweet
consonance
It isn't just your thoughtlessness
Or just your confidence
when I see you the words, I want to say
won't leave my esophagus
Your presence illuminates
I'll keep my love anonymous
Until you're ready for us to be prosperous

Limits less
Limitless
Feelings I get when I see you more
Talking less
Being more
This is what infatuations for
Departing
Has my mind wondering
What is this
No expecting
No deflecting
Somehow protecting
Me from
Expectation
Devastation
That sometimes is my situation
Please don't change unlike the moon
The seeds we have planted have yet to
bloom
Can't let myself get sucked in too soon
My heart lets me know my reward is
You

I've been a fool
I've been blind
Losing my cool wasting my time
Wasting my time
I couldn't see
What others recognize
Deep in sleep
Feeling traumatized
There's a point of falling
So deep that you don't know
What's up or down
I've been on this ride before round and
round
With no end in sight
Until I stepped out of confinement
There is an assignment
A journey
That needs my attention
Uncertainty
Doubt
Worry
And fear
Seem all the more near
Until I open my eyes
Take off the bandages
Step out of the lies
That I've told myself
I look out and see the world
Could be mine for the taking
But I'm debating
What do I do?
Where do I start
How will I know
I just have to begin

Jamal Roberson

Begin to let GO

You took me by surprise
Now I'm a little desensitized
To my failures in love
Because we fit like gloves
Each time we connect
I get a rush
Not enough to just touch
I don't want to just make love
In a dark tunnel
You are the light
Too intense to verbalize
That with you I'm so happy
I could cry
Not because you saved me
But because of the journey
That had my faith restored
In spite of my mistakes
There's an entry for us
To new love unheard.

25 Years to Life

Pain
Hidden from the eyes to see
But I wish someone could see
The pain inflicted upon me
Secrecy
Shame
Guilt
Memories
I'd rather forget
Again, and Again
Over and over
The shadows seem to reign
Tears to dry eyes
A time of having to say goodbye
I was too scared to say
What others already said was a lie
I bottled it up
I pushed it down
Further and further
But no depth could conceal
The damage I've yet to heal
Innocence
Taken without a second thought
Screaming but nobody's listening
This is how I've learned to deal with pain
Or I should I've been taught
To ignore the truth
To gag myself with heavy hands a heart
That quietly tore my soul apart

It comes
It goes
Still understanding
that I can't be demanding
To direct the flow
Just nerves
Anxiety
Trying me
Constantly
But I sit back
And play my role
The world made me cold
Because I had to play a role
Feed my desire
Take me higher
I search for answers
Forgetting
Knowing too much
Can be like cancer
It grows
It flows
If I'm scared
It'll show
Trust in me
In to me you see
You don't need to know it all
Just enjoy the process
And count your losses

25 Years to Life

Another Day with lack of solace
Pretending not to see what's been said
and done
Each time I think it's over you think
We've just begun
I'm so unsure of what we've become
Broken pieces I cannot make whole
Push me to keep letting go
Passion burning hotter than a furnace
Intentions unsaid, hearts mislead
Further I sink
Into denial
Words cut like machetes
Feelings getting heavy
Laughter feels so distant
Instances of betrayal
Moments of hope but to no avail
I'm vanishing
Away from the madness
Out of my chronic sadness

Jamal Roberson

I been through a lot of shit
We all been through a lot of shit
But I can't make you heal yourself
Was it because we're both broken, we
found love?
Even while apart we don't think about
nothing else but us...
Same ole story
Holding back
I'm keeping
Of how long I'll be waiting for the day
Where you won't be afraid
To be it
Don't think just be it
Just for one time
You could change the world
But you're holding back
Keeping track
Of this façade, this game we play
Being strong
For too long
You can't feel it
Just be it
Fucking cry
Just be it

I'm not your guy
I'm not the reason you get up in the
Morning
Just the one you let fly
And now has you wondering
Sold Dreams
Even though I tried to be by your side
Ambivalence in Abundance
Has us love deprived
I'm not the one crying
Too busy smiling
Healing
Feeling
Breathing
Believing
And dealing with my new chance
Created out of the circumstance
Breaking curses
That lie on a tree
Symbolizing family
Indifferent to petty mishaps and mistakes
Now understanding this is the course
Life takes
As we all vibrate
Higher than cranes
In this forever changing
Mental terra
Cloudy days
Bad fades
With blisters
Was the elixir

Jamal Roberson

For a meeting of superiors
With a passing glance all others

Were inferior
As grace and poised was he
A face I didn't recognize
But like the one I had fantasized
Of in my subconscious
While I was paralyzed to previous
Lacks judgement
Growth was stunted
Until I cleared a way
On a new path begun
Where love is genuine and reciprocated
Without malicious intent premeditated
Never worried
For he pushes past my fears
Learning to dry my tears
Like I can hear his heart beat
In the winter nights
Where we delight
One another
Intimacy
In to you
I see
A future
Brighter than the cosmos
That unites you and me

25 Years to Life

Above the horizon
Is where I like hiding
Thoughts and feeling gliding
As I unwind from stressors
Beyond my control
But it makes me feel better
Even if it's just an hour of my day
That I'm not bound to obligation
I didn't ask for
But I can't go back to how it was before
When the stakes were low
And the cracks didn't begin to show
When I get back on earth
My reality is as harsh as the pavement
That god created
Because my path is fated
To experience moments
Others can't even take
Because each moment of life
Is to be taken in stride
Because everyday someone loses a life
So, I go to the horizon
Only visualizing
In this reality
That's understood
But not mine
In totality

Agriculture
Foreign culture
Ignoring the torture
We've inflicted in crisis
I'm sorry that ISIS
Comes to mind
When finding time to ignore
The news
Because I refuse
To see the reality of a nation
That's lived two lives
Showing me beauty and expanding me
World
While watching the turmoil uncoil
At our door step
We're given freedom of speech
But we select leaders that leech
Off discord
We ban what offends our majority
While disrespecting foreign ethnicities
Abortion laws
All distract
That we aren't what we say we're about
Political warfare has turned into
Ego battles for clout
Turn away, make a way
But don't run away
You can make the change
But only within a certain range
I long for the days
That being an American is
Great again

Hierarchy
Perfect Family
Patriarchy
Expectations follow me
Poisoning our minds
For the world to see
A family trees
Whose vines have toxic roots
Infecting my mental
Limiting my potential
Breaking free
Will save the family
So that I can live happily
I can know what it means to be free
Even though we're family
It's feels hard to be me
Feels hard to be seen
Unless I'm wearing toxic values
With actions that follow through
Curses spoken
Destiny awoken
I proceed with caution
With fearful disposition
Moving forward without recognition
Not for bad intention
Wanting to bring my dreams to fruition
Am I being disloyal?
For being more vocal
I only think about my successors
Wanting to leave behind treasures
I want for them what I couldn't have
Which is life's luxury pleasures

Jamal Roberson

New beginnings
New chapters
Though it seems to me
You're unreachable
How could this be
Carrying hurt, injuries, mentally stuck
It's truly a mystery
Hurt and pain
Can't complain
Since I knew from the start
That we would eventually part
But we couldn't believe
Can't perceive
That even though this love is relief
We must concede defeat
Not that you didn't win my heart with glee
But that this Love was full of deceit
Without the truth we can't proceed
Reassurance is concrete
But we put on a show
Like we don't want the world to know
That we both let this love go
Potential waisted
Time fading
Because of love roles that are dated....

Percocet's
Popped pills
Foggy haze
Following cheap thrills
Fantasies of the mind
Chasing highs, feeling vibes
Trying to leave troubles behind
In a mirror I won't look
Too hard to face
Seeing tragedy is all it took
But the tragedy is my money
The fame I don't have
The love I can't make last
All stemming from bad memories
Of the past
When I'm high the powers mine
I feel like an emperor
The control never lasts
Sobriety kicks in
And suddenly I feel all the pain
All the weight
Of my jaded state
Dealing with my issues
Plays warfare with my mental
But I can't see the solution
It isn't crystal
Clear like it is when my state is altered
Feeling inadequate when you falter
I bury the pain, but it resurfaced
Because self-medicating won't
Erase what's my purpose

It was the same
Each and everyday
Until you changed on me
Claiming you fell out of love
You weren't the same
I stopped seeing your name
You started playing those games
Because you were afraid of love
An illusion of your creation
Scared to feel true pleasurable sensations
Now it just feels temptation
Now it just feels like temptation
Now you're on the run
Turn your heart towards the sun
Put down your swords
I'm not your enemy
Just the mirror for which you won't look
Acceptance is the remedy
A truth you won't accept has you shook
Keeping lies and appearances
Has you delirious
All the while you remained curious
Of the box you won't open

You fill my cup
Like a plot in the movies
Building me up
Never knew you'd fulfill my fantasies
Whenever, Wherever, However
I just need you here because you make me
Feel stronger, wiser and more clever
With a glance you'd have me light
Like a feather
A friend in you when needed
I can't call you only for fair weather
Since the day we connected I'll always treasure
When you show you want me?
Loving me more lately
Has me wanting to give you all the
Love from my pain
No longer can abstain
For my hearts a liar
You are my hearts true desire

Jamal Roberson

Monopolies
Atrocities
Hard to see
The monstrosities
Shootings in schools
Electing fools
Power plays for days
Trying to hide the true nature
But we've given ourselves away
Greed
Deceit
Characterize the American Dream
Hate watching the news
Because my heart skips a beat
Wounds not seen but, on the inside, I bleed
Working, living, and sleeping
In trauma is the way of life
According to media we just
Need some convincing
Not wanting to vote
Because political bullshit is
Never Ending
Hoping for the best outcome
Changing my fate
Due to a legal mistake
Is my greatest fear
Failing to reach my true potential
Is my nightmare
We can't change the world
But we can change how we will fare

25 Years to Life

Every time
Feels like the first time
In your eyes I surrender
Your touch feels so tender
I never want to hinder
Our future
As we move together
In love and grace
To safer place
Than our past
That didn't last
I'm not prepared but I'm ready
More prepared than the day you left me
But suddenly
You caught my heart unbelievably
Skin to skin
Makes me feel safe in the space we're in
Because of the way you tease me
Love is what I live for
And you love has me living grander
Than the nicest empires
Only you can trigger
My sleeping desires

Jamal Roberson

I bring balance
Where it's needed
Even if it's my own peace I'm not feeding
Even good people hit a ceiling
Codependency
Mediocrity
Is all I see in these unions
That continue to elude me
Broken promises
Left me broken hearted
Like a death when you departed
I know I was supposed to lift you up
When you're down
When you're not so sure
And while my love endured
It was your intentions that
Weren't so pure

The sun was at its highest
Temperatures rising
When I met you, I couldn't hide it
The spark in me
That was burning for you
At that moment I knew
My dreams came true
Not because you did right
But because you took all I
Threw at you
And yet
It was
Unrequited
It blew my mind
That we took time
Thought of lies
We told ourselves
And minds
That this
Was true

Jamal Roberson

Curtains closing
Energy falling
I know I'm intelligent
But never feeling I'm in the know
Fighting through my nightmares
With fever and uncertainty
With a promise that it'll help me grow
The air is cold
My heart is tender
Events unfold
And just like that I want to go
Away from this
Anger
Helplessness
Solitude
Drifting away from bliss
I remember the days where
I could laugh
I could dream
I could cry
I felt I could touch the sky
But lately
I've been feeling shy
Needing to escape
Because I need healing
From a world
That's injuring me

6:55
I'm awake and alive
Thinking of things that make me thrive
Thanking God for things,
He's never left my side
Routines, work and stress
Years from now, I'll be thankful for them
Nevertheless, it's a thorn in my back
Things I do that distract
Me from my dreams and hopes
As the world turns slow
My youth and ego also go
A new part and passions birthed
Old habits, idle relationships must be purged
To begin again
Remembering each day, I rise
That God still needs me by his side
For there's a mission unfinished
And I'm here to comply

Jamal Roberson

I waited for you
Waiting to
Be there
After all we've been through
Smirk that melts ice
Voice that melts butter
I shudder at the thought
No strength I could muster
In your grasp
I laugh, Smile, Inside
My heart hides
Is this time real?
Or another illusion
I'm sorry for your confusion
Waiting in partial solitude
Has weakened the trust in you
Not that I was rushing you
On your journey
I don't own you
The same way you don't own me
The patience in separation
Had me feeling moments of desperation
But I never grew complacent
Knowing that as I watered my plants
And they grew
You'd do the same
Together we'd reach full bloom
I haven't gotten the confirmation
But the connection causes me to start
Debating, Thoughts and heart
Adjacent
It can't be said
I'd wait for you
But if you ever return, I know

25 Years to Life

Who I would run to?
Through music I learned
Through music I grew
Through music I knew
Love comes and goes
It isn't always fun
But you won't know love until you've begun
To love yourself in spite of your flaws
Until you tear down the walls
Protecting your heart
Thinking we belonged together
My passion and love began to fester
Although there's separation
I know we're bound for the same
Destination
Through music I healed
Music gave me water for the heart
That began to dry
Although I can't see you next to me
Your energy pulls me aggressively
With lack of precision
Got ne feeling distant
I've waited for the instant
It all clicks and makes sense
Feel so intense
Love on the brain
Got me feeling ashamed
Am I playing myself?
Am I blocking my blessings?
Or have I not learned my lessons
There's only one way to know
So, we can end this drought
Leave the hiding, the pretenses
The facades
Just allow your true self
To come out

Jamal Roberson

Planning
Preparation
Anticipating
The situation
Bound to change the course
And forces propelling my life
No more poverty and strife
Dreaming of abundance
Never seeing my circumference
Was just an index
To greatness
I manifest
Generating my own wealth
Is my life's conquest
Codependency
Should be avoided
Making an impression
To be duplicated in succession
Is my life's mission
Using what I have
To get what I want
Inviting Karma, I can't flaunt
So that I may lay a foundation
For those after me
Hanging in the balance
So, let me do it alone
That's my soul's stance

You said you'll marry me
Saying that I'm good enough
You can't love
When your kin won't open up
Too much life has passed for it to be this way
I've been trying to get to you
Love on lock down
Love in silence
You can lead others, but you don't open up
Show up for you
It's too much work to do
For you to tell the truth
Counting me out
Through facing my shadow
Without a doubt
Only wanting you to display the love
You promised me
The admiration you gave joyfully
Had me wanting you incessantly
Facing issues
It isn't blissful
Playing with my mental
Wondering if I'm solving mysteries
Or creating vivid misery
I only have my faith in you
The same faith I know is true
With that faith I met you
Matrimony
Familial bliss
Awaits us once we endure life's shifts
I can't wait for an eternity we won't miss

Jamal Roberson

Where the sky meets earth
Fire and Air unite
Ironic that the sun lights my path from birth
As the dark depths surround me as I ascend
Proud, and Bold
With the need to be heard
Restless, optimistic
Maybe it's hard to stay consistent
But I work throughout my life on mental discipline
Walking on eggshells but more like unbalanced scales
Making an impact
Wanting to give back
Is what makes life feel purposeful
In union, equality
Is obviously
The only disposition that will
Bring our love to fruition
But we must both make that decision
All in my head
Is where my tension heads
So, I snap without focus
But I rebound by exploring my fall
Even as I daydream
Within heavy streams
Of the glitz and glamour of my dreams
In reality things aren't always what they seem
But it raises the question of how to make
Something that is concrete
In private
With meditation
I pray to God
For he prevents
My devastation

Concentrating....
I can't take it
I can't fade it
When you're gone my heart is breaking
Steady pacing
Are you okay?
Has the world turned you cold?
We're breaking into new worlds
Seeing our potential unfold
How did faith get away from us?
Let's not waste time doubting us
Give it all to what's above us
Faith and Trust
I know it feels we aren't progressing
But this path we're on is destined
For great ends
For new trends, big wins, flossing ...
We've been on a roll
Constantly on the go
But we got a long way to grow....
And if we don't try
I guess we'll never know

Dropping things
Freed from feeling on swings
I was blind to see
Bound to old mentalities
Non fulfilling ideologies
Wanting to stampede
But they can't proceed
What destiny
You see what's for me
Collective recipes
We're manifesting
No longer second guessing
It's time to take flight
And show the world our light

Under her rays
I have emotional displays
As she waxed and waned
My focus began to fade
Her beams pierce through me
As if she's always in my dreams
She never forced me to change
Just ask that I never remained the same
At times I felt at odds with her
Other times I'm glad she was softer
I'm unsure why I stopped trying
Even though you already surmised
Transformation felt unusual
But you were willing to learn
And I lost the trust I earned
In my dreams you always visit me
But I know we will never be

Jamal Roberson

Share my world
Share my joy
Be with me in my sorrow
I'll remember that while
I pave the way for
Better and brighter tomorrow
Share my dreams
So, we can fulfill our desires
As we live at the top like Supremes
As we love each other we feed our fire
Our hearts racing
In the heat of the night
As our bodies joined showing our faces
Sexual Liberation
Free from devastation
Our union is full of compassion
That will ensure our bond is everlasting

The world was ours
To conquer
And watch our fortunes unfold
Partaking in laughter
We knew it would be a story to behold
To travel but on more than one plane
Because our lives were forever changed
After we began monopolies
It never was the same
But the tools and traits were there
With domination for us to share
But even in the first hours
It was known, the bond was rare
The world was ours

Jamal Roberson

Could it be we weren't prepared?
For what was in store
Maybe I should've called you more?
I keep my poker face permanently
So, you can't see the euphoria
Emanating from me
Dark shadows have come and went
Praying faithfully restored my energy
When I was under the attack of the enemy
But nobody can stop is
Destined to be
Finding what seemed out of sight
But was starring right back at me
Isolation propelled transformation
Numbness came over me
Circumstances sapping my energy
Divine Timing
Birthed New Horizons
As I walked towards the sky
I thanked god for never leaving my side

25 Years to Life

The END

ACKNOWLGEMENTS

I want to thank GOD for helping me reach
a point that I didn't even know was
possible. I'm thankful for God giving me
the outlet to share with others through
something personal such as this. I am
thankful that I can give you praise for
living out your purpose through me. I
thank my parents for loving me, teaching
me, and supporting me. I thank my friends
that were cheering me on to finish and
supported me when I shared my poems
with them (you know who you are).
Lastly, I want to thank my brother for
helping me create the cover design for my
first book. I could not ask for more if I
wanted to.

Dedication

I dedicate this book to my mother for being the rock and the catalyst for me to explore this part of myself. The music you exposed me to early on resonates with me today when I get inspired to write. I am the man I am because of the woman you are and who you raised me to become. I want to thank my dad for encouraging me to go forward even when I second guessed whether or not this was possible. I thank God again for blessing me with the ability to live out his plan. I thank all of my ancestors who have come before me.

Made in the USA
Columbia, SC
12 December 2023

28367031R00030

25
Years to
Life

ISBN 9781695992771

90000
9 781695 992771